Prologue

When that old *musafir*,[1] the sun, drags his sweaty August face across the desert,
ducks behind the haboob's niqab that shrouds the flat-roofed cities,
swings his baggage across camel-coloured villages and shadow-crouching towns
where white and black, draped faceless, float over pavements like chess pieces –
he bobs awhile in the odd cloud, like a dhow or a caravel
puffed up by the Trade Winds, embarrassed to appear lost
before coming down to land, to start another moony season of wandering,
only to drop off the edge again, like a stranger who has never been,
perhaps afraid of too much attachment or of not catching another Trade wind,
or maybe just trying to escape the heat of his chains;
does he ever think if his comings and goings tell on the faces of those he leaves behind,
or hear the questions at his back?
"Where you been floating this time *Musa*?
You see anything worth talking about? You change any histories?"

He is never sure what he should say, is expected to say, or to be that he isn't already,
so, he blurts grandly instead:

"I am all *Musas*. What else can I say? I have no name and no face of my own.
I am a pilgrim of the wrinkled palm and the silver coined mirages of the sea.
I am just a wanderer, here to tell my story.

It is what I have left to give."

---

1. *musafir* – Arabic for "traveler" or "wanderer"

Notes from the Dream Kingdom

~ A Story of Migration ~

K. G. Goddard

Illustrations by Beth Jeffery

Second edition 2025
First published by Botsotso in 2025
59 Natal St
Bellevue East
Johannesburg 2198
botsotsopublishing@gmail.com
www.botsotso.org.za

ISBN:
Print: 978-1-7764952-8-3
e-book: 978-1-7764952-9

in the text © KG Goddard
illustrations © Beth Jeffery

Acknowledgments

Grateful thanks to Sheena Goddard and to Beth Jeffery for their readings and comments. Also, thanks to Allan Kolski Horwitz for his insight and editorial work.

I dedicate the work to my family.

Cover design & layout: Beth Jeffery
Design & layout: Graeme Arendse

We journey towards a home not of our flesh.
Its chestnut trees are not of our bones.

– Mahmoud Darwish

Without her you wouldn't have set out.
She has nothing left to give you now.

– C P Cavafy

a direction is never lost
like a man moving east to west
huddled in thin light, in a hermit's hut –
well-battered spoors lead like arterioles
into a man's home – his heart.

– Mxolisi Nyezwa

I
East of East

1

He arrived in the dry heave of the Arabian summer, slid over
the cold sweat of the airport floor, fell into the bazaar babble of customs,
the ragged lines of hopefuls come from the edges of maps,
the shuffling indentured, peddlers of luck and prayer beads,
bagging their bits of flotsam from the teeth of the carousel; and with them,
he passed finally through the weary exhale of the airport doors;
and strode out boldly, naively, into the dawn's carbon slap,
hailed a bearded taxi in his suddenly alien language –
> a stuttered haggling for a ride to God knows where,
> some scribbled address an hour down the road.

And all the while, the sky kept its niqabed face closed,
and its thousand eyes only blinked their questions at him:

> "Who the hell are you? Why are you here?"

On the road, the traffic lights were a scatter of feral eyes still not chased off
by the sun's swat that would soon rise out of the sand
and throw the first flat hand of the desert at the window,
the final reality of the days to come, hitting his face:

> "But since you're here, let me show you the actual shape of desolation,
> the real Gulf. Not that slip of sea you're driving past –
> the one inside the time-stopped hole that's made its house in your gut.

Stop your dreams of the south.
Take this new life, another kingdom of dreams.

                    It has roots thick and sticky as tar
                         to sip away your memory,
            and leave you days so full of sand grains
                   you will not know one from the other,
                            and be soothed."
     "Time Kill," he discovers: ticking hours,
until ticking becomes your breath, strange and intimate to him as his new name:

"ajnabi" – foreigner

◎ ◎ ◎

On the drive, the paling sky is silent; the line of the horizon is a mirage.
The old driver's hand pumps to the sound of oud and daf, guttural chants
from the radio; and as the rickety Corolla lurches into dawn under the heavy tap
of his sandalled foot – the grey beard, the torn thobe, stained shemagh –
                    both sink into an inarticulate muteness.

In this light, *Musa* cannot decipher the road signs, though some are in English:
    Al Khobar   Ad Dammam   Al Dharan,
          Ras Tanura Al Qatif Al Hofuf Al Jubail

All strange as moon language, strange as the old classroom stories he remembers –
with their smell of chalk dust and the warning fingers of teachers –
                         stories meant to be taken seriously:

                  "God is in them, listen!"

Miracles in the desert: water coming from rocks, seas parting,
blindness healed with mud, bloody crosses – or stories of white heroes
of the Arab struggle, Lawrence, the pillar of wisdom.
    "All men dream, but not equally," he said.

They were visions to the West, throbbing with the intimate wiles of a harem.

None back then spoke of the real strangeness: of oil refineries with lights
like Christmas trees and tongues of fire puffing black carbon into the air;
or the wailing of muezzin from minarets stretching into the blue,
declaring five times a day, a miracle: faith and oil, born from the sand.

        Is it true, *Musa* wondered, as they came into town,
    that miracles need a desert to come to pass,
            or is it only a mirage?

II

Was it some kind of miracle or just the same hole that his ancestors found
in that salty swirl of surf that clicked in the throat of the 1820 shore?

Africa, dark, bristling with wild sounds, less readable than the stars;
the eastern Cape's hieroglyphic face; the bend of Algoa Bay's white bone
snapping at them in their landing boats like hot teWeth spitting past
their still soggy thoughts of England . . .
        words they could not decipher, but whose meaning they knew:

      "*Hamba kaya!* Go home!"

The bay's jawline echoed the open mouths of the watchers they took for savages,
    "unbelievers," a name they stole from Arab slavers: "*Kafir.*"
They planted themselves, made the place a local habitation, gave it a name,
and became "*Umhambi*"[2] – the unwelcome, the feared, anviled there in the feral scrub

---

2. *Umhambi* - Xhosa for "traveller" or "wanderer"

of aloes and prickly pear and sun-burnt, waterless rock; their new iron age
surprising them just as this sun-white northern sand
                              now surprised *Musa*.

The green breast of the Cape bared its sap's promise.
They lurched for it, loading trinkets and muskets and bottles.
But not even the shires of Bathurst fed them enough, or gave a farthing
for their prayers.

                "Nothing grows here, you lily-white fools!
        Don't you know they lied to you in England, they could not read the land?
                    Its face looks green, but its body is stone,
                    Pringle knows, riding off into the veld!"

Only cows and sheep dribbled around the pock-marked hills that squatted,
like crag-lipped old women squinting anger, pipes smouldering,
pendulous breasts swaying with too much history,
ticking off the days, months, years, centuries . . .
                        Waiting for them to leave.

The stone-age rock at least welcomed them;
bits of flint left by the *Strandlopers*, the Khoe and San.
If they had ears, they may have heard the First Man's ghost
whisper from the painted caves:
                "Be like us. Use only what you need.
                Live, but don't inhabit. Let the veld be your speech,
                        its gifts your wisdom."

But they made themselves the First Man's keepers,
settled, planted their heels.
Home is always at the root of blood.
It throbs like a whip in the heart.
And they lashed its hole there and it engulfed them.

In it, they spun their new iron and wheel world around those stars they wanted to see,
              an image of the old –
     as strangely familiar as the southern cross: the promise of a gold sky.

They named the place, Port Elizabeth, after a dead woman;

a ghost roaming among the chants of Hindustan,
looking for her sad groom, still grieving for his bride,
who would never hear its waves or stand on Fort Frederick's hill,
and watch the sun cast shimmering dreams across the bay.

Now those waves, washed, dressed and redressed in white for two hundred
blood-worn years, break over the bony *dolosse*[3] stranded
beside the highway slicing the crouching town,
while a sea of tin shacks rippling the red edges of the poverty-doused sunset
              stares down any who look it in the face.

The steel arms that grew from the graves of those lost at landing –
or lost in the hundred years' war of the frontier – swing over the harbour, Gqeberha
     (the ancient, Khoe name dug up at last from its forgotten grave).
They bend to service the gaping Chinese ships that swallow the cars assembled here,
then cough them out, gleaming as polished horn,
     to satisfy the swell of desire across the Mandarin sea.

---

3. Concrete structures on the beach to block sea surges

Behind them they leave smouldering light, bulbs of Tik, stashes of "buttons,"
and a million blades tattooing a million arms;
    these same arms half-descended from those who trampled the bush,
      stole the cattle, harnessed the natives to quarry the stone and build the houses
   that still gaze out, like stranded sailors, over the bay;
        the silver sun spilling its sea-coins, a pirate's loot,
    for bits of the promise they came to find in their grains of sand.

Their new world would be rusted cannons exhumed from *The Sacramento*,
    blue-eyed dark natives descended from *The Grosvenor*,
the salted lives of slaves drunk with wretchedness from the beached *Dom Pedro*.
And through their stories, the past would still only blow like the call
   of a lost albatross into the white shore.

                Just another settler's salt-tale . . .

What's left of all those might-have-beens rumpling the bone beach,
    while the stench from the black stacks of Swartkops coughs into a future
   congested by a thousand Boesman and Lenas bickering about money.

It slices the air between them like the concrete freeway slices the town –
        now mostly potholed, and wind-slapped;
like those Saturdays when the South Easter blows away the soul of the old city streets,
when even beggars hanging near the traffic lights head for the bush
to sleep off their *babalaas* or douse their hunger with meths;
their bits of washed rag cloth draped over fences and bushes like flags of surrender;

their bony expectation of plenty sunk along with the other three hundred odd ships
        whose skeletons still moan in the deep.

III

The deep of the northern desert is its surface, an endless horizon,
a mirage hiding shapes that *Musa* comes to know of but cannot see.

    "The desert you see, is the desert you want to see," it is said.

But what can an *ajnabi* see here beyond surface?
Bare sand breasts the gulf's break between scowling continents:
        Saudi/Iran   Arabia/Persia;
ancient brothers in arms, joined at the hip like twins
suckling the same sun-crusted blood-milk;
    scowling Cain and Abel, Gilgamesh and Humbaba,
        Sufi and Wahhabi, Shia and Sunni –
           the chaos of the old dance of night and day.

Among them, *Musa* seems only a pale exotic;
another curious alien "native" of English, a mad dog
walking at midday with his cap and bag, as foreign to the locals
    as the natives of Africa were once to him –
        a beggar, not unlike those odd one
    or two wandering the old town at night, after *maghrib*,
        risen from beneath the surface like sandfish:
women with hands and heads covered, husbandless.

    "Two riyals for my children *habibi, barak Allah!*"

They are mere shadows in the shadows now that their husbands look no more
upon them; and their hope is planted in human courtesy, in *caritas*,
    accidental as a fiver on the pavement.

Even in the rich north there are beggars, wispy and faceless as the southern ones;
those who used to knock at the paint-peeling Grahamstown doors at dusk
when he, young enough to gush liberal guilt, listened:

> "Ten cents for bread chief!"
> We are poor chief, but you need us.
> To shoulder your wealth joyfully, let us help
> you cast off the burden of disgrace your wear.

And he, like most others, gave.

> Who ain't a beggar? Who ain't a slave?

◎ ◎ ◎

Now he has come north to sell his tongue.
It drips rounded vowels like torn money bags,
spills its strange fruit in high-tech classes,
drops its southern syllables for them to hang their impending futures –
> jobs, cars, child-bulging houses.
He is their guide and their manservant, their admonisher, their cleaner, their coddler.

> "Lick arse if you have to *boet*,"
> says Jason of the Joburg Argonauts
> (long beached here to extend his fleecy years).

His mantra is simple and universal:

> "As long as the green river still flows,
> and the bank account grows."

He loves the obedient boys he commands, every lesson sharp and ordered as a march;
every day ticked off like a neat-soled accomplishment.

Musa, soutie of the PE Souties, crawls through the trenched maze of corridors,
his white skin and his titles are his flag; his labour, the arms
he has surrendered to the rows of downturned faces.
Strapped to ideas brown and wrinkled as the khaki they wear,
they play the game of learning, pretending the green river is not
what keeps the corridors flowing with flannelled legs,
shiny shoes and the same different faces every new year.

The coat of money has become his uniform, thin as paper but endlessly durable.

> "If you cannot be part of a country," says Jason,
> "then at least let it pay you for your service."

They have become like the servants of his childhood.
Like Compress, the gardener, machine muscled,
edging flowerbeds to perfection every Saturday;
or coughing, shy Paulina, who would die of kidney failure,
polishing floors, dusting sills, missing her rural children, waiting
for the madam's eye to shine.

Here, the northern overlords, offer *qahwa* – coffee – sweet red tea,
medjool dates whose caramel is said to sweeten loneliness;
all God's gift to the faithful, the true, but only if they obey,
if their words are His words and the longings of their hearts are His longings.

The palm at the end of Arabia is an open palm, but its blade is sharp,
and its word is armoured as an unbending trunk.

❀ ❀ ❀

Like all *ajnabis*, *Musa* learns first the weight of *In'sh'Allah*: maybe, if,
when God wills, it will happen, when I, your master, the servant of God, feel ready;
then of *shukran*, always be grateful, it is the will of God and it pleases men,
then *mafi mushkila*, no problem, the best way to be liked by the master.

Soon they fall easily from the tongue. But like the servants back home,
they, the *ajnabis*, know when silence is best,
to be wary as the goats and sheep offloaded from shit-stenched ships at Eid al
Adha, sensing what is to come, what they are there for –
                their footprints, their faces, their words, their uncovered heads
all consumed and forgotten as quickly as last year's herds.

            "The global village," says Die Kaapse Klopper.
       "We came for this, so don't complain if this is what we get.
             Everyone's house but the home of only a few."

Maybe this is what the old settlers thought, huddled around their strange new hearths,
backs to the crackling winter veld outside, all those eyes like spear blades
                          waiting in the dark.

He sees those eyes in supermarkets here.

              "What you doing here, *ajnabi*? Stealing the oil,
                grabbing all you can get before running?
            See, you cannot even carry that overloaded basket."

"Who the hell are you?" he wants to say, "It is your children I teach."

But he bites his tongue.
Never dare question those who question you.
You are the guest, the honoured white.
The honoured never step from their honoured line.

Durban Curry laughs.

"You know, there is what you want,
there is what you need,
and then there is money.
Money can tie itself around your neck
and make you a donkey.
We are all donkeys, my bra."

They honk agreement over their shakshuka,
tuck again into the plates set before them:
their babaganoush, their humus and their tamees.
There is a word Africa has taught them: *Asinimali*: "no money,"
mafi flus here, a phrase only the rich need use.

"Home is not where the heart is, or even
what you make it," says Durban Curry.
"We should not lie to ourselves.
Home is where the money makes its home."

"Remember Ibrahim?" Says Kaapse Klopper,
"that old Bangla gardener who, after thirty years here,
couldn't afford to attend his wife's funeral,
and hadn't seen her for three years before she died!"

They remember a leathered face, wind eroded eyeballs;
a dirty shemagh swaddling a grey head, baggy browns in forty degrees.
He could not remember the feel of his wife's skin, her hair, or the smell of her food.

        "Take all you can get, then get out home,"
            Joburg Jason says, scooping humus.

        "Make your fortune, even if it is from dirt."

IV

"What is fortune?" *Musa* wonders, alone in his bachelor room.

Is it made only from compression and pain, like pearls or diamonds?
And when it has finally been made, is it so much dust?
Surely the one not a mirage, greater even than the brush of a beloved's skin
against the cheek at midnight, is to no longer desire fortune?

        How not to be a beggar? How to want nothing?
To be free of this life of deferment, the self-made gulf rounding
            whatever the eye thinks it must have;
    the barrier, like Ibn Arabi's *barzakh*,[4] creating its isthmus ache.

But in Ibn Arabi, the *barzakh* is the meeting of light and dark;
the still point from which all other points diverge and to which they return,
like all the days of the past and all the nights of the future:
           the cycle from which none escape.

Musa hears its hole in the chant of the muezzin at dusk.

---

[4] Literally, "barrier," but in Islam also the stage between death and resurrection.

"Rub away the grains you fear so much and let what remains swallow you.
Fall into that gulf, then you will lose the desire that binds you."

But who really wants to be unbound?

Don't the Bhagavad Gita, Plato and the Buddha all say
that in the hole of this cave we scratch at imagined walls,
and cannot even see the gulf surrounding us though we feel it there?

Gilgamesh came to this very coast for this, to visit old father Noah,
Utnapishtim, Lord of the Flood, and dare to cross the Deep as no man would dare.
He crossed the River of Death, found the Flower of Life,
turned for Uruk, but lost all in a drunken night.
                                          Lost the Flower
and had to live with Death waiting on his back
stuck between the cave walls of his illusion.

But who really wants to escape the illusion? Who really wants to escape the cave,
and outrun death?

"I will not be a failure," he said,
"I will make home my reward, and these lion skins I wear show my virtue."

So, he returned to his ancient doors, his family and his clan, to begin again.
His bed was his children's laughter, his roof, the warmth of his wife.

"Cut the crap," he knows his friends, *die manne*, would say.

Gilgamesh

"Have you ever been really poor?" Joburg Jason would ask again.
"So poor you ate the quinces left on the tree
and had only empty hands to show your children?
Only the well-fed can look upon money with disdain
and turn it into philosophy."

Musa is silent.

He sees Gilgamesh walk away from his lost Flower; and he sees the beggar woman
sit silently, head bowed, on the evening pavement downtown; so tired of asking.

"Never claim you can live without begging," Jason says,
"and never be ashamed to beg. Begging is the work of faith."

Kaapse Klopper laughs like a minstrel, swings his polka leg and his clown-bell gaze
across the room like an old banjo:

"Ja, broer, God gee alles, en alles vat hy terug.
Eet vandag, maybe môre issit net geloof wat oppie tafel sit."

V

It's true here.

Belief decks the table even if the table is just a Mac 'n fries.
It pumps its breath through the arteries like a coolant to keep the desert thirst away,
the social engine running. The morning's *fajr* and the evening's *maghrib*,
and all the calls between; the drawing down of shop blinds,
the unrolling of prayer mats in corners everywhere;

the cries from minarets keep the towns, the cities, the schools, the factories,
and all the shadowed people in them, obedient machines, comforted.

Only on the roads, on the thin, black blades of tar,
do they, the wild boys, test the fading freedom of their youth,
believing they are immune, or Allah will take them if he wishes.

His wish is their wish.
If not, then marriage, jobs, high-walled houses, kids, *masjid*.

◎ ◎ ◎

Down south, in the African veld, time and faith are measured,
not by mats and shop doors, but by food. Belief is food, and food belief.

"The Lord will provide, even if those thieves – the government –
have stolen the future from the mouths of our children."

Faith is a corrugated, wind-bent hunch over a paraffin-fogged *umngqusho*,[5]
wrinkled anger stirring a thick-burnt pot.
Faith curls its wafer under a threadbare sheet and waits to see if tomorrow hunger will
have gone to hunt children in another shack.
Without fire there is no faith, everyone knows, but it's also true that a fireless house
can burn faith to ashes.
How strange that it so seldom does.
Here the grandmothers sit around the stick-thin flames in the eyes of forgotten children,
leftovers of AIDS, TB, COVID, stolen child grants and runaway fathers.

While in the treacle-rich north, the angry heat breeds mostly hooded faces
and more and more "*In'sh'Allahs*," that tightly knotted word muffling the wails
of the mothers of the eight thousand and more children dead on the road every year.

---

5. *umngqusho* – Staple Xhosa meal of samp and beans

In the north, that father rules the tar while young Ahmed lies spreadeagled in a crucifix,
                one eye popped out, books flung to hell,
        bicycle wheel still spinning its last empty seconds.

Or the children flying like little angels across the highway from their bus,
              a last, permanent detour after school.
Or Ibrahim answering his mobile on the bend to find that it is Allah calling.

      "To Allah belongs the dominion of the heavens and the earth.
              He gives life, and He takes it."

In the south, it is different, but the same:
thirty years of "freedom" and the black diamonds and the white diamonds
      still keep the sea of silver-sunned shacks locked in their circle of faith –
            fattened by gold ringed fingers and greased with promises of a smile.
Death is not only the mother of beauty, it is also the father of faith.

        Faith is Noma shot in Zwide for her phone.
      Faith is Uyenene, raped, bound and boxed in a post office.
          Faith is pregnant Tsego, hung from a tree.
      Faith is Zakariya who died running from child gangs.
           Faith is the six-week-old baby raped.

        "The Lord giveth, the Lord taketh away."

Faith lays the table with words for the unspeakable.
      It is not an answer to a question.
            It is the only meal left to be eaten.

                  ◎ ◎ ◎

But there is another question *Musa* and *Umhambi* must answer,
not unlike a death and a faith dropped like a stink bomb
between rows of desks and the lecture benches;
the north on their marble floors and polished wood,
the south in their red-brick fort, propped on the hill's Vista over the noon's silver
salt pans of "Sun City,"
      Missionvale's mirage of a lake district.

   "Why father, teacher, do we need this English?
    What is wrong with our own language?
    Are our camels and our cattle and our histories not enough?
    Is the black gold Allah has given us not thick enough?
  And the gold of the mines our grandfathers died in not wealth enough?"

Here it is – the hot, stinking question of the new faith: globalization.
The boys' northern gutturals are earth-deep,
sure-chested as their certainty at being The Chosen:
the world beyond the desert an irrelevant map.
They toy with its shallow show like they toy with another video game,
a "Call of Duty" or a "Minecraft" or a "Fifa Football."
Allah is their Protector, their Word, their Fortress.

And in the southern wild, between the Veeplaas tin and Zwide's smarty box houses,
      who needs another language?
Do the knives and guns not speak a language clear enough?
     Can a stranger's words fill the empty stomach?

Umhambi has no answer but the one he was taught: the Empire will die,
but the global language will be here a long, long time.
It sucks dry the words of any who disagree, and drops the queen's tongue
    in every mouth like the promise of a crumb.

◉ ◉ ◉

If we could learn from the past, what would faith be but another dusty book?

No more Sharpevilles and Marikanas;
no more "The Child Is Not Dead" poems;
never again Biko's corpse in a van,
or Ibn Battuta's maps and Ibn Majid's compass recalibrated in blood.
No more Da Gamas scrounging in the gold sun for India –
    Algoa/Delagoa/Goa left faithless
      with only his trinkets for hands and a dry tongue.

These northern tribes need English as much as the first Xhosa needed
the ghost-coloured strangers rising from the snake-dark sea,
     home of the slithering sea people,
come again to break, the legend says, a hole in the wall,
         and steal virgins for their randy king.

  "Take this tongue," *Musa* tells his students.
  "It is my gift to you. It may taste of poison now,
  but without it there is no food and your children
  will be left with empty mouths at the dumps –
  outside the global village like the rest of Africa."

"Sho, Sho. True," they nod in Missionvale; "*Ma'sh'Allah*", they defer in Arabia.

But the slow poison devours *Musa,* too, just as it covered *Umhambi* in dirty white.
The Englishman, brushed clean in his own history books, sought across the world
to make others at least look, if not be, like him and his works made by faith.
He sprays flattery, his toxin, over them, like a farmer sprays his crops,
      a priest his prayer, a cat marking its territory.

They pay for every burst he has to give.

"Help us teacher! Help us!"

Black holes opened wide for him,
the unrelenting mirror he is condemned to see afresh every day.

VI

Once, like them, *Umhambi* walked like a prince; once, he said he knew God,
heard Him walking in the garden at evening,
saw His face on street corners, felt Him in his own breath.
He promised mothers that their dead children were in heaven.
He told old men how to live, to be humble when their gold shone,
to love when their love seemed to be ash.

They listened below his fresh-cheeked pulpit with upturned, generous faces.

His mothers and fathers, old as the servant making his bed, shining his shoes,
   sweeping the dust of his bedroom floor, washing and ironing his clothes;
old as the wives and lovers of the men he saw on vacation work in the mine
hostels, when he strode like a white lord in the compounds of a thousand mine workers,
   platooned far from home, drilled in the sweat-burn of underground blasts,
bone shaken, dragging out the belly's innards for pickings up above
where the white gods sat, waiting to stamp their pluckings with the mark
of everyone's futures.

In the compounds, eight-beds to a room, sulphur stench still hanging on them,
the rock-blasted faces sat impassive as tin soldiers,
eyes faraway as the lone kraals on the hill they called home,
tongues silent that in youth had clicked to call the cattle home at night.

To the white boy wandering into their way, hidden thoughts like bare-knuckled teeth,
the *stompies* on their lips were half-lit fuses that became, once a week,
on Sundays, a whistle, warrior chants and gumboot dances,
  slaps and hardhats and bellows, Johnny Clegg *Indlamu*,[6]
to catch a faraway memory, and knobkerrie thrusts to scare an enemy away.

Their hisses were staged, but they were the same that would fang
through the '80s and '90s with their petrol breath, their matches and their tyres,
fingering *impimpis*[7] – man and boy and woman –
surrounded, charged, sentenced, and Firestoned to ashes.

Faith in the fires of freedom.

> "Come and see the mine boys dancing, aren't they so cute?
> You must see them at Christmas, so lively and entertaining.
> You can get a glimpse into real kraal life."

Around Boy Scout campfires the white boys sang their half-envious imitation:

> "I cumba zimba zimba zi-o
> I cumba zimba, zimba zee.
> See him there the Zulu warrior.
> See him there, the Zulu chief, chief chief."

For a firelit moment in the veld, they were warriors too.

---

6. Zulu War Dance

7. People accused of being "sell-outs" during the anti-Apartheid struggle. Sometimes they were "necklaced" as punishment – petrol-filled tyres hung around their necks and lit.

In the outdoor showers the miners laughed when they caught him
in the surprise of his own gaze – at the baobab legs, the trunk arms,
      unreadable histories like the rings of trees rippling through their torsos,
      and appendages that swung in lengths he had heard were mythical –
in time with the promise of their bicycles' tick, tick, tick as they wheeled
into the backyards of white houses where their girlfriends, freed from work, waited,
letting them forget, a little, wives, mothers and children unfed in the kraals back home
      and the rock faces they had to face again next day.

Out of the steam they came like ancestral ghosts risen from the red ground in cages,
      waiting for their faith to bring fruit, for their time to come.
                            And for some, time came too soon.
It coughed them up limp, rock-crushed, to be slapped, prodded, measured and dumped
in boxes, then sent home to their mothers still waiting for the next envelope of money.

  "Big dicks these men have, but don't be fooled," said Piet the compound manager.
      "Big dicks don't mean big work, or clever minds.
   And don't be surprised when these boys overturn their plates and their beer,
     or fuckin complain about not eating the fish and pap we made for them.
        It's just who they bloody are. Savages."

How did a nation come to discard itself, *Umhambi* thought back then?

What brought them to these caged barracks if not their own disbelief
that any other human being would take the trouble to own them?
      Freedom was not yet an idea to be defended against a small band of ghost-white
      marauders, blood-faced as Cortez and Columbus.

Only Nongqawuse really knew, the little witch girl a stone's throw from Salem:
to escape slavery, the slave must give up what is held dearest –
>
> the fear of being forgotten.

Dead cattle packed the land like the miners a hundred years later would pack
the mines with labour, with winsome eyes and machines.
For faith to grow, for a few distracted tribes to become a nation,
and to emerge from the mist and from the fires underground,
it must first become nothing.

VII

Here, the muezzin cries his Nothing at the sun;
burns the evening moon hanging in the palms into an emblem,
a stamp of the hand of God. And in the millions of sand-grained faces
bending low and rising, like the sun or moon, and crying and bending again,
making their constant cry, their unquenched chant, their echo of certainty,
there is a bend and roll constant as the white waves covering the desert –
round and round, like the circle Hagar walked searching for water for her son,
Ishmael, moving forever towards home: *Al Kaaba,* the *Bayt Allah,*
> calling all bodies that thirst,
> like the moon calls the tides.

Few here wish to escape the roll of faith: where would anyone go?
What does a different, faithless world have to give?
What is this thing "freedom," about which people speak, as if free will has meaning?

> *Fewer drawn blinds, more choice of brides, more, or perhaps less kabsa?*[8]
> *Different cars, different houses?*

---

8. A favoured Arab dish of meat and rice

In the unending summer that Allah has given, there is no need for spring.
Only the forgotten Shia of the east, bunkered in Qatif and Bahrain,
exploding tweets like cyber bombs,
        coming into the classroom after nights of boot-broken doors;
    brothers dragged from beds, sit stonily at their futile desks,
            eyes blank and pitiful, plundered by too much sight.

Faith here is a two-handed God: one of white fleece, the other, tooth red.
Eighty-one heads once lopped off in a single day:

        "My people only understand the sword," he, the One,
        tells world leaders, with a Netanyahu grin.

At noon on Fridays, "The Voice" beams a sword from the minarets across town.
Its eye arcs over the palm groves lining the effluent river like brown blades
    standing to attention before the houses hunched near the banks.

It catches the disinterested, the sleep-mossed, battening behind their cryptic walls.
It tells them they are protected, and who would argue on their carpeted floors
                decked like Roman feasts?

    "What do you do over the weekend all of you?"

        "We sleep teacher. And we eat. What else is there to do?
        Sometimes we go into the desert to hunt or barbecue;
        sometimes we visit family or play computer games.
            But mostly we sleep."

        The eye of Faith pins them in their rooms.

It was the same Eye of a different God whose army *Umhambi* saw in his youth,
slicing its search light across the hollowed gut of Grahamstown,
the small Settler town huddled in the dark veld
before Mandela's raised hand brought some sun again.

Makhanda's spirit still walked the streets, though on Christmas day
the year the Settlers came, he'd sunk centuries before in the shark-toothed rage off
Robben Island.

Umhambi would not forget the Ratels, and the hurled stones seeding the roads
like fuseless landmines; children's bombs, and the pale, green faces of helmeted boys,
their trenched heads protruding from behind the Ratel walls, wheels whining
down Raglan Road like Stukas, ready to boot through Makanna's Kop, the old shack City
on the Hill, older than any soldier's memory of his ancestors, tougher-skinned
than any Great Trek *riempies*, more leathery than any stories of boer heroism
they had to listen to in school.

> "The more you try to kick down the door of the idea of freedom,
> the deeper your boots will plant its tree," someone said.

But they booted anyway, green with numbness, tight-faced with obedience and fear.

"Kill first, before they kill you."

In the north, the palms, like the spiky headdresses of quieted warriors,
glow orange in the night lights along the river,
obeisant even after the day's loudspeakers are silent.

But at dusk, in the half-light, when the beam from the *masjid* light is broken
by the glide of pigeons, dropping from roofs through the darkness,
their wings dipping and rising as if in a prayer of their own,
bending their heads on landing in quiet contemplation,
                        there is, even here, a strange peace.

It seems unkenned, like that first stop of silence after the last incantation,
or the unplayed chord hanging in the air like a fermata,
a hand for the other chords to hold; or like the eternity between clock hands
                        giving time its beginning and its end.

          Without order – even the pigeons know – there is no peace.

Yet what is order without the wind rattling the windows?
This is the yin and yang of it, an easy old conundrum to live by.
How *Musa* wishes he could share the evening chant's peace,
the chained chaos of a cathedral song, a *masjid* dua;
hold the rise and fall of its bar like a father holds his child through life.

But there is too much reason lying in the way, like a child's bombed body.
It blocks him in the street with its cold, callous smirk, and punches in the gut –
that yearning to collapse into faith's infancy again.

                    "Be like a child," he says to himself.
                    But the child lies dead in the street.

So, he is lost in the babel after evening prayer as it rolls down King Abdulaziz Street,
    after the momentary brotherhood of haves and have-nots in the *masjid*;
  before the last ameen, and the poor, come from a hundred other countries,
bowed in glad thanks for their pennies, shuffle out, and the rich come to their Lexuses,
       their Cadillacs and Mercs, waiting outside like footmen.

The robed and kurtaed crowds flow past the Sharq Hotel, the fluorescent gold shops,
the greasy, dust-sandalled workers clumped around Western Union,
breathing in the oil and curry air, exhausts and tobacco and Urdu and Tamil, and Hindi,
Bangali and Amharic and Tagalog and scatterings of Arabic,
                                  shouts into phones at far flung family –
  these men of the four corners, these men of faith and salt and desolate houses,
carry the most ancient of mines in their eyes, in their grey beards and in the years
           of longing grown sticky under fingernails.

    "If you dig deep enough, work long and faithfully and hard enough,
                you will come to the promised land."

             No blade of reason can blunt that belief.
Every shuffle of a sandalled foot every payday, every wife's evening call,
every coy answer excavated on the phone from a half-known child,
every breath of longing from an ageing mother,
                becomes another step into the black hole of faith in Time –

           Time that will take the migrant home.

VIII

When *Umhambi*, pale and sweat-blanched, first turned off
Stanford Road into Beetlestone, past the cemetery,
past Gelvan, the Coloured area, past Helenvale, the gangster zone,
into the daffodil names, the green valley names,
                          bestowed long ago by the still-pining settlers,
he laughed dumbly at himself,
            the skittish laugh settlers must have heard in their own mouths,
               of the stranded who cannot quite believe the beach
                  they have come to is real.

The rock, the thorn tree, the aloe, the mud – brown as the skins
of those they met for the first time on the scrubby shore –
spat at them like the bush-dust spat its korrel, and looked at them
with eyes as flinty as the voices the fearful mothers used to warn their children:

> "*Hamba* – stay away from those whites,
> don't be fooled by blue eyes and friendly smiles."

Those blue eyes must have been to the Xhosa and the Khoe, he was sure,
more foreign than the moon, though soon to become as intimate to them
as the blood that flowed in dongas and kayas, down grassy knolls,
not yet become streets.

> Makana blood. King Hintsa blood.
> Blood in their veins.
> Writing history in red.
> Always red.

"This is not yet England," white mothers said.
"Keep away from those *kaffir* children or they will taint you with their savagery."

> And still the blood flowed, veining a nation.

◎ ◎ ◎

Here, in Gelvan and in Korsten, Brutus, bushy haired, bok-baartjie poet,
strode the knife-strewn, corrugated pavements like a Roman,
> before banishment to Robben Island's shale.
And here Nortje exploded his paper bag of poems, thumbed his half-breed dogsbody
at those riding past – the lift that never came – signed off his literary history
> with an Oxford overdose and a Korsten cupboard's scribble of brown papers.

They bequeathed the leftovers to the Helenvale, Gelvan and Korsten poets who
rap between the bullets and blades that beat out blood on Saturday nights,
> "Tussen die gangs en die Tik",
>> smoking their brains to pot before the knives come,
repeat what the Khoe did with dagga, long before *daai witpens* Van Riebeeck
>> took his first drag.

It's one way to escape from the workless hours,
dragging their hands through the empty kitchens of another day.

> "We are a nation born of alienation," *Umhambi* thought,
as he entered Malabar, the little Indian estate on the hill that seemed
a forgotten droplet from its northern mother's breast,
>> ten thousand miles and histories away.

The squat houses of Gelvan turned their faces from him as he passed.
The storied few of Parkside turned up their noses, puffed out their chests.
> The poker-faced fruit-sellers ignored him.
The broken streetlights looked away, ashamed for him with his white-boy goodwill.
> The tin roofs flashed their rust-stripped teeth.
> The graffiti on the walls gave him the finger.

For sure, Malabar's patched sari was not the golden bead of the Indian shore
Da Gama aimed for when he sailed past here lashing his bull-ship north,
fashioning the imagined silk of his new world with whips, golden crosses,
trinkets for the locals, and offerings by fire to his God,
> like the Moslem pilgrims on their way to Mecca in the *Mirim*,
> burnt alive to prove his Christian piety.

◎ ◎ ◎

Here, on the wind-lashed eastern coast, a mile from where Van Der Kemp,
even before Hintsa was dead, had walked among the Khoe with his freed-slave wife,
and preached the kind of equality that made Brits nervous, and Boers plan their Trek,
the *masjid*s and temples and churches clutch together like orphans
                    still wearing the off-cuts of a fraying faith.

Their dance is silent, like a wedding couple in an arranged marriage,
not sure of their steps around the fire, but gathering the folds of all that history
they must suddenly weave into something new – braided stories, tip-toe tongues.

Umhambi, carrying his white Free State history like a caul,
arrived at the Eid table of his lover like a newborn,
and let them finally pull it off so that he could breathe.
He sat before the dark-eyed bride like a plaintiff,
a groom come to see if he could actually be the chosen,
could be allowed to savour the mixed-coloured feast;
an explorer wanting to have his first bite of a dapple-creeded life.

           He was roped by the four-corner spread.
           He was a navigator with a new compass.
           He was a prodigal getting the fatted calf.
           He was the new son among nodding, bearded fathers.
           He was a boy speaking an unknown language.
           He was an orphan who knew he was not home.

IX

Woman, do you remember the froth of the white waves in the wind off Humewood,
there on the beach spitting prehistoric spume in the pier's face?
"How dare you intrude here?" it said.

And then, after the storm's rage, how the sun would lay its soothing hand
across the bay like a mother's returned from a long absence?
And to settle the spat, shake the white spittle and the black bile coming from the belly
to a tranquil silver stillness, as if nothing had happened?

Remember the black cormorants hunched on Spear rock out at sea,
too wary to come into shore; and how the white gulls spreading their wings,
rose and dipped above the messy shore like untouchable lords of their demesne.
How both you and *Umhambi* said you would never be like them,
either cornered on an island of the past, too angry and afraid to launch off,
or glide too far, out of the reach of the churn and spatter below.

"Live with the rough you are given, make of it a tree to anchor you,"
you both said.

Memory is always too late.

Maybe it was the fire that came to lick the red-brick walls
where the bougainvillea was sticking its thorny nose through the roof,
after licking off the bark from those spindly little half-naked bluegums
in the veld that you both thought so rustic;
the fire that burned the place clean of snakes and frogs,
and curled the young yellowwoods planted
in hope at the far edge of the lawn, into black twigs.

It was meant to be the child's garden, for her to roam in
away from the hiss and spit outside.

But history always remembers; it never stays hidden for long.
It hangs secretly under the curls of lips and explodes before anyone can control it.
Its fire was inside and outside, family fire, race fire, woman and man fire,
us and them fire, you and him fire.

You both thought you'd tamed history
with some kisses, brick walls and a child,
but you only brought its rage out from under the sea.

◎ ◎ ◎

Umhambi and his bride and their child found, faltering by the shore, the real desert.
    It lurks in the heart.
    Heartsblood colours the world's desires,
    pulses it red.
This time the sea was no mother to come soothing,
    but a fire that cooked Malabar's seethe,
melted Welkom's stubborn mechano-head of iron.

    "You little men, you little privileged whites,
    whining lily boys, silver spoon boys,
    tables laid, beds made, shoes cleaned,
    shit wiped, snot wiped – man up!"

But he fired back:

"And you, bloody black feminists, all you do
is indulge your victim complexes, play the same boring blame game.
Forget the colour of your skin and what's not between your legs for a minute.
Try real equality and see what it feels like.

Grow up!"

The brown brick, the white grass, the little fist of bluegums;
the fire-blackened wall, even the books smelt of smoke, the smell of grandmothers
refusing their grandchildren because their religion was wrong;
of grandfathers not knowing where to put their pasts and their suddenly,
strangely,
too-pale hands.

So, the half-built edifice falls, finally, like a loose painting from the wall,
already tired of itself, memories too exhausted to fight themselves anymore,
leaving a shamed mutter at the door,
"I will see you soon,"
muffled by the flat slap of wood in the frame,
fooled only a little by the small suitcase,
but shocked by the empty driveway,
the puzzled dogs waiting for their walk,
the trusting child on the marooned stoep,
the mother beached in her shipwrecked room.

And he, bobbing in his small, unkeeled hovel, a prelude to the rudderless north,
a worm slowly turning into its *Musa* moth,
in a chair whose stripes would mimic the gelid brand of an Arabian room,
spume-hot bars of anger, shame, black-choked logic frozen,
drenched in the lie of relief.

❀ ❀ ❀

After that, no more ordinary evenings in Port Elizabeth,
no more commonplace houses "composed of ourselves."

        There are only foreign houses.
        There is only the before and the after.
    A place and time once imagined has become nowhere,
and all *Umhambi* does from this moment forth is mere compensation.

Not to take the place of the dream lost,
    or to stitch it back in a new pattern,
        or indulge a pilgrimage of disgrace.

But to learn that the marriage of opposites – fire and tears, water and air – can spawn,
if he is circumspect, the Real in the Imagined.
        And without the fire and the wave,
          without the constant surge and tumble of the ever-changing,
            there is no relief.

X

In the air moving north or moving south –
    sometimes it seems the same thing –
                is relief, and not relief.
    A bipolar life,
like the sun in winter – warm but cool,
like colleagues met in corridors and on street corners,
warm but cool, never giving more than is circumspect:
        friendship, *zadik*, *maatskap*.

Among the sojourners in the north, friendship is picking
through the days like prayer beads treasured,
pocketed for the next time, forgotten in the lurch for the door.
To grow too close is to open a hole too wide.
Huddle instead with family, pine for those far away,
let distance be the thread that binds.

And in the air, when the horizon's golden thread drops off under the port-holed wing,
hangs the dark continent from its end like a mystery all over again,
and only the firefly lights of small towns bob in the black below,
like unmapped stars, how can the world not seem to the traveller
                                              to be upside down?

Foreigners have become friends, and friends foreign.
Still, in this bipolar movement, there is a strange kind of homeless contentment.
Musa and *Umhambi* can both allow, for now, this conditioned air to breathe for them,
the plane's lung to keep the pipes open between what was and what is to come,
the sky self and the ground self – it hangs above Africa's burnt bone
and the furnace of the Middle East and leaves them in mid-fall.

A kind of peace – some other hand is here to catch, to fall into, for a night.
In their falling – brothers and aliens – their two halves become ever-separate twins,
the air self, floating, and that other self,
the one born to foot the red soil below with jelly legs.
The two are one, but always, one part foreign,
one part being, one becoming, while never quite knowing which is which.

                              ◎ ◎ ◎

And here, as the golden thread of dawn and the earth's dark sword
become clear outside the portholes, coming down the aisle, is Virgil.
Pushing her cart through the circle of their limbo, she brings stories:
the same old stories the philosophers tell to keep their fears from spilling,
bottles of logic to silence gluttonous questions, warm cloths to soothe
turbulent thoughts; food for greed, and entertainment,
the last of the stories, to imagine another world, an escape.

All know they will never be satisfied.
Even when they stand ready on the tarmac, one foot first,
then another and another, moving but discovering for the umpteenth time,
they do not know who or what controls their feet.

> "Forgive us our blind feet," one will say.
> "Forgive us our deaf hands," one will say.
> "Forgive us our stupid tongues," both will say.
> Even half believers must ask forgiveness for what has been done
> and can never be undone.

In the north, Ishmael the Bangla taxi driver waits, dripping sweat and exuberance:
  "Welcome home, sir. Sir, had a good vacation? Sir, ready for another year?"

In the south, the waiting train sighs; the sun is rising in both easts.

XI

"In the north, there you'll feel free," someone said.

No more southern fears in cramped rooms, barbed wire dawns, high wall sunsets,
barred windows hiding the face that in the mirror still looks like a face
                                                  to apologize for itself.
But if *Umhambi* thought to see a different face in the north,
                                  he sees only a different mirror.
Its language is foreign, but its words swing the same blunt sword:

"Apologize, *ajnabi,* for daring to look with eyes that think they know what they see.
        The mysteries of the *arabisk* doors on our houses
        are as hidden from you as the faces of our women.
        Our windows are papered over just for you.
        Our walls are as high as yours down south, to keep you out.
        You will never understand our culture or our politics,
        so leave your liberal shit at home."

But then he walks by the river at dusk – not river,
but an effluent tunnel spilling chemicals from factories into the sea.
It glows in an orange light like a shawl of formulated tranquillity,
shared, for a moment, by the last of the sun and the first of the moon,
like the two eyes of the heart Al Arabi describes:
                the imagination joining dark and light,
                as if the *barzakh* between night and day,
                the laws dividing the seen from the unseen,
                          are suspended,
                and time is stopped, and all places become one place.

Around the river the Terns, come from Europe and Africa, duck and dive
over the bowed Egrets arrived for winter from the north.
                      It is a homing place, a place not out of place.
The smell of barbecues, the shouts of footballers,
the whoops of veiled girls, rollerblading,
are windows into worlds otherwise never seen.
One Other seems little different from any Other,
and the evening is dressed mellow as the Free State
Saturdays of his childhood where the braai smoke hung over the veranda
like a white shawl drawing everyone into its arms:
                a peace that seemed never to require understanding.

Then, in its still-green imagination there seemed no smell of evil,
in the white-rinsed news, no word of the black burnt bodies at Vlakplaas,
no TRC to dig up the graves from the manicured lawns of apartheid,
no wails of the widows before cameras, or Nomonde Calata, or Tutu crying –
                no statistics of hourly rapes and murders.
It was then like the north is now:
        no whispered stories of migrants slaughtered near Yemen, in their hundreds;
        no stories of violated maids or executed grandmothers;
        no talk of crucifixions in parking lots.

In that world, when darkness fell across verandas,
              it could still be a prelude to a vision outside time or place,
          the touch of something or someone beyond an ordinary hand's limits,
          like the moon and the sun in the same red river where the birds
                    would continue to come, year after year,
the children continue to play, and lovers walk with the pleasure of smoke in their eyes.

Can it be this smoke is the Cloud of Unknowing –
                  what the ancients said was where God is found?

S

N

DILMUN

A place without place, a word without words,
a silence that is also a luminous darkness where knowing is overshadowed by loving,
                 and both exist only in the light and dark of the Other,
           loving what none can define.
      Or could it merely be the black Veil of human Will?

"What you don't know, doesn't hurt you," Joburg Jason says at his braai by the river;
he never listens to the news, never lives beyond his means.

      "No," *Musa* thinks, "I have known something more. I know I have."

In the golden Free State veld at sunset where the kiewietjies screeched
in their final rising and falling for the day as they had for thousands of years,
                                       he knew it.
And sometimes he knows it across the dark light of the moon-glowing desert
where the camels and pale-lit houses have come to rest,
and the refinery fires and house lights glow against the orange sky
as if they are the only speech necessary.

      And for that moment,
                      love and desire,
              what is felt and what is imagined,
             what is needed and what is known are one,
           though none know how and have no need to know.

XII

From the Bahrain causeway, where not long ago the tanks bullied across
                             to slap some protesting Shia faces,
the lights of the island flutter in the sky like an orange sail in the sunset
as they have for thousands of years – under Persians, Sumerians, Assyrians,
                  Babylonians, Portuguese, British and now Arabs.

The island's dark hull dips and rises with a pirate's promise coming out of the mist.
Its Siren call brings young and old over the causeway to the pressure valve,
the uncorked steam whistle, the same promise of paradise that legend says
brought Gilgamesh to its shores thousands of years ago –
        Dilmun, the ancient Flower of the Sea.

For those who come here now, there is the rifle of passports,
of baggage in and baggage out, checking for contraband,
knowing glances and hidden smiles, in taxis and from border guards;
and, at the end, where the murk explodes into the glitter of hotels and bars,
golden showers of cars and neon flares – Circe awaits.

She is Chinese, come to make money for those in the village at home;
she is Russian or Ukrainian, come to escape those at home;
she is Filipina, come to another island, to find rest from home.
She is all things to all men, a drifting flower, looking for the arms of forgetfulness.

Musa has come too, with his comrade drifters, Aussie Rover and Irish Clover,
underworld guides, who have seen it all before, done it all before.
From the Gulf Gate Hotel, they slouch through the back alleyways
where curry smells and bangra music squeeze through greasy doors,
between creased kurtas and the sweaty armpits of vendors:

   "Ten dinars, sir, imported (from Indonesia) shirt sir,
    twenty for Italian pants (from Bangladesh) sir,
   Bollywood DVDs, only ten, special price I give you,
     and I give Qawwali CD half price."

And if you whisper the right questions, hashish, or a girl, smiling, biting her lip,
brought to your room.

"Only fifty dinars gentlemen, cheap. Still fresh."

The three slouchers come to the feeding trough of Diggers
where the white-bloused Chinese girls are spread across the long bar's bower
like translucent silk bundles.

A band throbs on a red-lit stage; luminescent arms suck men into the trough
like lost sailors.

The girls' mouths gape. Some plead, some hiss the oldest incantation:

"Me, take me!"

They clutch at arms, buttocks, sleeves.

"Watch your wallets, lads," says Clover.

They are mostly replicas of the woman-child *Musa* finds beside him before he can sit,
her hand in his like a butterfly, opening and closing its wings;
her cheeks alabaster under the neon; her thoughts cocooned;
her hair a faraway float of black silk.

They cannot speak. This is not a place for speech.
This is only one of her preludes to a life still being born:
faded sheets, drawn blinds, sticky nights.

Then the stale dawn of a requiem.

◎ ◎ ◎

She has the look, *Umhambi* will think later, of the sunsets over Hillbrow,
when he, in his lushing, came to sojourn there;
the neon faces floating down Pretoria Street, and Twist and Claim,
                                      and returning again, and again,
to trudge around Highpoint, like circling a Capitalist Kaaba,
immune to the smells of piss and beer, not yet watching for the knives
that will come out later, after midnight, or listening for the gunshots
that will wake them in their beds, make them roll over,
                        alone or into the story of one maybe just met –

    "I was raped last year, you know, and all I got back from the police
            was my soiled panty with some stains on it.
              You won't do that to me, will you?"

Here at least Wanda – with her pale blue hair and gold stilettos – can still explode
like a Persephone from the dark cave of the Chelsea;
and the piano above Mi Vami can still swell its soothe
when only the wind and some stray beggars under newspapers curl
                                around thoughts half-formed –

    "What to do now, with Time?"

Thoughts broken only by the trash, carried out from countless silent flats,
and with it the bodies of the night's dead;
            some from overdoses, some from stopped hearts,
              some shot in their beds while still asleep.

                              ◎ ◎ ◎

In Joburg's dawn smog, the hooded silhouettes of lonely buildings
become naked again in the sun just as in Bahrain's sea-strewn haze
the skyscrapers appear like sails from out of the dark, breathe a sigh of relief,
and flap their designer butterfly wings.

And the wrappers of the same question blow across the streets below:
in the city of a thousand paths that twist the choices any wanderer makes,
            and after a thousand years of wandering,
why does the same street corner with the same scrubby feel, still lie at his heel?

            What must he do with it?

            It is the past and the future.
            It is what he sought to escape
            and what he sought to find.

            And it is what he has never left.

XIII

There must be an end, a coming, with no more going.
                                              Sometime.

So, when, in the early Ramadan, the moon outside
                Musa's and his new Persephone's (his Kali's) window,
hangs its crescent wafer between the blades of the date palms planted along the river,
        and the muezzin cries at dusk and dawn for sustenance in duas of regret –
            duas begging forgiveness for deeds done and not yet done –
and looks up into the darkness for a harbour to welcome the wandering soul
come by its secret star across the desert to the shoreline,

he watches her standing again before her lamp,
a small yellow flicker in the dark,
at which she whispers:
"A*um Sai Ram,*
Aum Sai Ram,"
and folds in the secret letters she leaves for *him*, the other one, the one before him,
become one of the gods now,
in the land of her memory where he cannot reach,
no matter how many moons he watches pass.

He has come to know there is never any having –
only the borrowing from some mystery of brief times, and briefer places.
Here, in the flicker, is the divinity that shapes their ends and their beginnings:
the indecipherable Sense felt in the blood and on the breath; yes,
and touched only by the outstretched fingers of dreams.

And here is the collection of prayers:

the "*Aum,*"
the "*Allahumma,*"
the "Redeem me Oh Lord,"
the *Shema* – the Lord Your God is One,
the "*Aum Mani Padme Hum*" –

all prayers for the eyes of those not there,
and always there,
the long gone and the newly arrived children,
and the children's children –
their southern breath threading north into south,
and south into north.
And all the world into a single place.

◎ ◎ ◎

It is the story of fathers who did not know they were meant to be the Sun,
                                        and of mothers who are the Moon.

In the south, the moon is a trickster.
It plays tok-tokkie with the wanderer's feet, eats them
like the Kalahari mantis eats its mate.
It glows, red and orange and white over township roofs,
gives hope and breaks hope.
Leaves uncatchable shadows so the Sun chases it forever.

In Northdale, the moon sits in the trees watching where the old man,
Persephone-Kali's father,
props his arms on his rickety gate, and gazing at the white town below,
                puffs out his rage quietly: a Sun, going down.

Not unlike *Umhambi*'s old man, puffing at his Free State gate where the moon
hangs blank, ever-changing, but leaving nothing changed,
he, too, draws on a rage he does not understand but which he has lived all his life:
                        how to live a half-controlled, half-understood life?

In the darkest moment of night, the moon's forgetfulness silvers the veld,
quiets the day's birds, and all the families are allowed a shadowy peace.
From its silver they take their promise.

                It is gentler, more hopeful than the day's sun.
                    In its shadow, they can hide.

So *Musambi* – that is his new name – now has a new, lunatic history,
strung between the stories of strangers who are not strange: white and brown;
God of Sundays, of roasts and cutlery,
God of Fridays, of biryani and moong and roti, and right hands;
                         and gods of all days, three hundred million gods,
     sitting cross legged over pots of dhal and rice and temples of incense.

            "I am more than my history," he says.

But the moon is silent, cold as the old man's feet he touched
before the fire took them in Northdale;
cold as his father's forehead before the fire took him in the Free State.

            When he tries to read it, it slips away.

On their bed, Persephone-Kali, come from the dark, from another time,
stretches out her limbs, tawny as fresh earth,
        a gazelle, too skittish still to be home, too beloved not to be.

Once, their touch straddled the gulf between continents; and the stars,
like the question marks in their parents' and their children's eyes,
                               kept their place.
Now they no longer think of different continents, or eyes that are Other.

There is only one place where all the gods, all the continents, all the languages,
                       have no distinction from the Other –
the place that holds the look of love between those who see the moon
                         not as a shadow for hiding,

nor the sun as an eye from which to hide, but both, in the Other's eyes. And so, interpreting its time and distance is of no matter.

Ibn Khaldoun, walking in his Tunisian desert, called it "asabiyya."
It is the breath between generations, the union of place and time,
a desert rock spouting water, mud; giving sight to the blind.

It is the one sand grain among millions that is never lost, because it is always lost,
so that it can always be found again.
It is home because home is no place, and no time, and no breath.
It is the wind that waits for the wanderer to cease his search.

Three children

11

The Marooned Stoep

1

(First Child)

I remember how, in the dust and weeds drowning the vacant lawn after he left,
the stoep floated like a loose raft in the veld, past the bluegums, looking at me
like people look at a lost child:

>What you doing here, girl?
>Where are your mother and father?

Their barked trunks were undressed, alien, a shock of white,
bared like disheveled Sirens just woken from sleep,
>in a strange country, surprised by their own voices.

Their white skin could not be hidden, any more than mine
under all those *Allahs* and *Ma'sh'Allahs* falling from my grandmother's lips.
>How she liked the lightness of my face!
>How she worried my face would taint my faith!

"Is faith the colour of a skin?" I once dared to ask, "or a place of birth,
>or a language, or some cloths over the head,
>or a dua, or a certain kind of food?"

In the veld, floating on the fatherless stoep, I could not see what faith may be.

Perhaps it is something you fall into when your feet cannot find the ground,
and they must wait instead to be found, like on Saturdays
>when the car's engine revved up the drive.

But what is faith when you are stretched
between the brown mother arm and the white father wave?

I touch the ground and it slips from under me, like he slips off at the end of Saturdays;
like she slips off behind her closed door when he is gone.

◎ ◎ ◎

I am more than them.

    I know this, even if I don't know how.
    I have learned it in the mirror
    that's looked me in the face
    since my first morning's memory:

"Here, this is your shape, your colour, and this the cadence of your voice.
Take, it is our gift to you, you are unique."

But the mirror is never only true.
        It is always too much and never enough,
    a prison window for Narcissus.
   Where to look, then, for my own story?
What else but to step off the stoep, let the waves of the veld take me,
   walk on them, forget fear and sink into both their stories,
      and make my own from their mud?

Mandala

II

(Second Child)

"Aum Sai Ram, Aum Sai Ram"

This is my chant, my Time, my lamp.
This is what was before my father and has come after him – gone
       with the ashes in the waters off Swartkops.[9]

       Too far but not far enough,
memory's life still caught in the lungs like smoke, near, but not near enough,
still sitting on the couch in the Northdale[10] concrete house I was born into,
       and eating at the table of the mousey Mthatha flat we fell into,

Bush College girl squeezed bedrooms glued into the brown cough of Transkei dust.

Torpor seeped into the walls, poured out of mouths that bit themselves.
    Flat hands. Ashamed of too little to offer.
        Days of gifts, sparkle and toffee days;
       and days of brown brood.
And always the wrinkled face of the land that always left the same question:

    "What the hell are you doing here in this godforsaken place?"

"Learning to hate ourselves, as the nation does,"
       was the answer we laughed about.

---

9. River in Gqeberha (Port Elizabeth). In Hindu funerals the ashes are usually poured into a river, as in the Ganges, a symbol of life and regeneration.

10. The Indian Area of Pietermaritzburg

They were split by the battle against self-hatred, my Rama and Sita.
                              Still, they were there – always,
                      except when he was gone,
                            for times and times, and then back again,
                                      and then gone again.

And then, one night, just gone. For good. Or bad.
                                    I no longer know.

                    So, what now, in this desert of my mother's new room,
            after the waters of the Swartkops
      where we neither sat down nor wept?

After the ash that floated into that strange sea?

                      ◎ ◎ ◎

Who is this strange man with his blue eyes and paste white face in her bed?

                    A wobbly, over-bellied misstep.
                  Step, they say I must say.
                Misstep I say.
        He dares. But scare, he won't. Not me.
                      You can kill a father, but you can't kill memory,
          or what could have been, or what was yet to be.
                      The memories grow in me like a green dream,
My *Aum.* My centre. My beginning, as it will be my end,
                          the end for which I know I was born.

        I will let it grow inside me till it is born and fills the future all over again

so that I can nurture it, protect it, keep it from harm,
    make the world into what I am sure it can be:

              bigger than a mere country,
              more lasting than a father,
              present every morning,
              still waiting every night.

              My universe, my *duniya*.

III

(Third Child)

    I am nothing but myself, my own man.
But I am also always more, and also always one:
                      a staircase of winding stairs,
                a room of clutter and peeling walls.

    Mirrors offend me – they don't tell the truth.
              They don't see what I see, what I hear:
          the voices talking, telling me their secrets,
          taking me into their room.

Not that *baasie* father with his worn-out jabber.
Better to break the mirrors so everyone shows their true selves,
              double faces, a hundred eyes split,
    like the country.
    schizo, like me –

Illusions

black and white, *makwerekwere*
with their jittery bush faces,
wrinkled *outas* and boers and *rooineks*,
everyone's black eyes watching everyone's black eyes
like the people here in Happy Home who drag
their cracked mirror faces stupidly
to the TV every day, all day,
then carry them up to bed at night.

It's fucked up, to be one and not one.
But that's the country we live in.
The Russians are coming!

Looking for a father, like the *tik-rookers* looking for *tik*.
But what father is there?

Safer to stay inside, man. Hide
from the ones who say they are your fathers –
those split lips, those two-tongued smiles.

Which tongue is talking now?
The real one or the pretend one?

Like the wind down in Govan Mbeki outside,
the this-way, that-way laugh between black-faced buildings and empty windows
where the *tsotsies* sleep.

You never know which way it's blowing,
or what colour the face will be next;
what the *tsotsies* will do.

The Russians are coming!

My father the *tsotsie*. Rich *tsotsie,* too.
Cracked bricks for cheeks. Hooded,
broken-eye windows. Waiting
to knife you if you don't watch him carefully.
But don't worry.
I spot that grin,
light and bouncy like the beams from the cars coming down Russell
on a Friday, flicking at the *straatlopers'* legs under the lamps,
at the red lips walking *los* at the park gate, and on the *tikkers*
and the *nyaope* dealers down at the Donkin.[11]

The cars float by on Saturdays like used shopping bags.
Nothing to be sorry for.
Like mothers who don't have to ask why they made us, the unlovable.

Stay inside.
Don't show them how much they wish we were gone,
and the fathers don't have to ask why they walked away from us.

Stay inside.
Don't show them we know.
They don't want to know that we know what they don't want to know.

I hear their voices in the radio, and in my head.
Their real voices. Hating. Afraid.
Especially of themselves.

Stay inside.

The Russians are coming!

---

11. Elizabeth Donkin memorial.

IV

(First Child)

Sisters are the vine on which tomorrow's fruit hangs.
                         They can bend under the weight of neglect,
     carry the forgotten years like a stored harvest ripening in the vats,
          be ready to be opened when time gives permission.

         But I do not know where my sister is,
                               and there are no vats.
      Perhaps there will be other vats and vines,
   a tree like one I once saw growing among Roman ruins we visited,
        where "I love you" seemed caught in the leaves,
               not lost in the echoes of stone walls.

She is my step – my misstep – as I am hers,
      my diversion to a foreign land where our separate ancestors pushed off,
                 to come here;
     one Hindu worker, one Moslem merchant.

        Our unconnected stories tell each other.

She is always either behind me or in front, straight-backed as the Red Fort in India,
      masked and agile as a Kathakali dancer.
          I have never mastered the flute for her dance.

      The old Roman ruins I once saw were mere stone,
   stones fallen from old stones, lingering in the grass, comfortably abandoned.
     But their essence was as it had always been,
         touched by youths in their gaiety,
            by gladiators in their last entrances,

      fondled by girls in love –
        vines for the imagination.

I imagined us walking there, me and her,
       becoming familiar with the etched and weathered blocks;
     daring to touch, to feel two thousand years
      between the fingers, shared,
    like sharing the face of a mother
   who is no longer there, but whose touch still tousles the mind,
      whose stroke is still in the blood.

     But if blood does not make sisters,
  how much less does mere marriage, or the urgency of a stepfather's will?

     They are foundered pillars overgrown by weeds.
    Though their past can never block
   us from wanting to see ourselves
      in the face of the other.

      ◎ ◎ ◎

In the ruins of sisterhood lie the stepparents' mockery –
        they want but cannot always have,
    want the step to be more than blood,
   like a faithful climb to the highest tier of the ancient, unsettled
amphitheatre of desire, something resonant,
      old and always new, steps lightened
    with the effort of wanting, just wanting
   – please love one another –

                          leading to a rounding, a full sky of blue
        at the last point of reach,
            where from the top, far above the stage
you can catch all the whispers,
                pick out your child's voice from a hundred others,
        and be happy that there is nowhere else to go
            but down into the cacophonous play.

        This is what they want, what they think is their right.
            But how it slips by them,
            how it gets lost in so many voices.

V

(Second Child)

        Mama, here's his face again.
Here's the love-lilt and the shrill of that Janus voice, those Agni eyes – in her.

                      The dark-light.

Even in the cot we saw him in her: the same surprise at the white walls,
            the plantation shutters, the forms that shape days and nights;
      the same umbilical Will to cut those shapes away,
                like nulling whatever imprisons.

I fear she will make her own way, as he tried to do,
            flinging embraces and vitriol like he did, unshackling toys.
              In the end it strangled him.

Mama, I need the clean flex of your arm, your eye's gravity to stop me
fixing her to a room to keep her safe, to let the shutters stay open, let the sky break in.
Let me breathe and not suffocate from fear for her.

How did you do it when I was her?

◎ ◎ ◎

My love, there is only a little I have learned from love and from ash –
even *vibhuti* daubed in the temple; even from the cracked urns
                            and emptied bottles of milk washed down rivers.

       There is in loss, only loss.
                            It gives nothing in return.
Even when the sun rises with one of its Mandela smiles,
                   or the new baby cries only for food,
                            or the morning chorus of the birds begins.

What is gone still lies in the pit of your stomach, like an unborn twin:
fathers worn smoke-thin as flailed aluminum;
husbands drained and ulcered in the hospital bed;
Edenic childhood houses bulldozed in the Group Areas,
the grassless, two-eyed pondokkies allotted the displaced;
the shamed eyes of parents, the bent shoulders of neighbours.

       All those years working in the dark mills,
                or pouring stagnant words into forgetful classrooms,
    climbing mountains of scripts, brushing a daughter's hair,
            scrubbing floors and cooking for her and others to be satisfied –
    all this is never enough for the twin.
It will not leave you be.

So, if in her new face you see his lost one,
or the great hole of a craved peace that is in you,
cotted in her wide eyes,
>>let her be.
>>>>She is her own universe.

>>One day she will become just another person,
>>>and still leave you with the old question:

>"How do I love you, my twin and not my twin?"

VI

(Third Child)

Father, though you are not father, just the black hole of a memory,
I sometimes wake up to that rain falling on your leaf-decked house in the valley.
Don't think it softens the brick plastering over that look in your eyes,
>>>>the one we grew up with.
It always looked past me, to some faraway place, a dark moon place,
>>>>>floating away, where I was not.
>>I think it must have been Russia!

>We watched it sail across the waters of your face, right through us all,
>>and it broke our bones as we clung to you.

Now I am a stick man, bone man, rattling (the psychiatrist says)
>>>in my story's cage, too scared to escape.
>>No, I am not brain sick.

I am bone sick
in a bone-sick fatherless country, where we have all become what we hate:
broken bones, beggars hanging on traffic lights held up by those looking for flesh.

And you, just like all the millionaires gliding in their government cars,
their blue lights, their flickering tongues, sipping on your leafy decks,
dropping a few coins for the old women in threadbare lines on pension day,
you are the black open mouth whose promises we have to fall into to survive.

You must be from Russia!

Oh, my captain, you don't know it, but you are the captain of bones
in a country of skeletons.
When will you stop sailing away?

◎ ◎ ◎

Father, if you see my mother, tell her that pale moon eye of hers at night is offensive.
She peers through my window and smirks her white teeth at whatever I do.

I close the curtains, but she still looks.
Can't even jerk off in peace or listen to my voices on the radio.
She hangs in the branches, like a trapeze artist:
one night here, another night off to Joburg;
a wisp on the phone once a week,
breaking my bones with her tongue.

When she dips her moon face into the sea, she drags me in,
drowns me in her radiated, mechanical light.
I am a lunatic, they say.

But I can still shine:
my bones shine like X rays at the bottom of the sea,
my fish-eyed skeleton dances on the seabed of my room.

I wait for the Russians!

VII

(First Child)

From Malabar's hill, my grandmother often looked out across the crouching hollow
of Gelvan and Helenvale,
the child gang, knife-ruled streets at the blue hook of the bay,
to a wish she could not speak.

They said it was a marriage hole, or a lost son hole.
But I think it was just a history hole –
the black, angry pit all Indian women
then were born into –

"Be silent and serve" –

who found herself, after so many centuries, washed up here,
on this wind-grit life.

Her hands were cracked bark, leaf-thin; her cheeks, a worn pot;
her voice, in the end, a faint north-easterly from a foreign past.
She thought she saw her lost boy's brown eyes in mine,
even if the whiteness of my face was not his.

Violet

Violet

Violet

Violet

Violet

Before she went, she gave me her hole, like a cherished bangle.
I keep it now for memory, to remind me to breathe.
It cuffs me to the silver chain of the bay,
the same bay my father took off from against his ancestors' wake.

          Am I not, after all, the sediments of all their journeys?

      All my escapes keep me rooted to the same place,
        even if I never fully know what place it is,
      or which father and mother and grandmother
          I will find when I search for them.

               ◎ ◎ ◎

Father, hole of my hole, even when I sit beside you, you are in another place,
even when you show those old pictures of us, you are a visitor's yarn.
This is what chains us together – that we are both salts from a strange sea,
        night-hulls touching and parting,
           then striking out again to search for each other in the mist.

               ◎ ◎ ◎

Daughter, loved, hull of my hull, sail and keel and rudder,
there is no wind without you, and the bay eludes me.

          Your hole is my wind.
It drives me madly over strange seas and keeps me whole oceans away.

For I am Diaz and Da Gama and Camões, and Ibn Majid looking for their ports.
I am the floating slaves of the Meermin sailing by their unstill star.

It moves, like you, from the child on my shoulders,
                licking ice creams on Humewood beach,
           to the woman now sitting across from me at the table.

I can't separate these moments into any kind of progression.
They are still, but never still, time unmoving, but never the same:
a revenant in your hands, resting on the cloth, folded around your cup.

            I have no answer to its question.

All I want is what every worthy father wants, hunts his whole half-legged life –
           the fathomless touch of mutual love and regard.

It is like the flower you were named for, wild and blue,
                  a scent for which to cross oceans,
          to dive whale deep into the darkness beneath our stories
              and bring them into the sun –
     and perhaps, if I am lucky,
          to be set free from their fear of themselves.

           Put your face in my hands
            so they can have shape.
           Lay your regard at my feet
           so they can have purpose.

VIII

(Second Child)

Father, what is the language of ghosts?

> Is it the words I sometimes hear beating like an old *bhangra* in my blood,
> the *geetmala* on my tongue, my *kabhi kabhi mere dil mein*?

> Is it the dance my feet move to because I feel your feet lifting mine?
> Your feet are clearer than memory, and more certain than imagination.

> But I still wait, to feel you again.
> What is it that I dance?
> How can I understand what I hear on my tongue?

◎ ◎ ◎

Child, my Shiva dancer, my light,
what can I say to you that you don't already know?
You are the dancer of my ocean and my dust,
the feet of my walking with the ancestors,
> the song that I lived to sing and did not,
>> whose footprints disappeared in the waters off the Swartkops.

I have come to rest in your blood and in your feet.
> > > This you know.

I know you hate history lessons, but it is not your blood or feet alone, or mine.
Our blood was in the ships with them when they crossed the *Kala Pani* – the Belvedere,
the Truro, the Pongola and the Umvoti, and all the three hundred or more others –
though so many of our footprints were lost at sea,
and again, after we landed.

We baked with the rats in the cane-field sun,
we spilled years in the slime kitchens,
we became spectres at masters' tables,
their *dhobis*[12] at home, and their *sepoys*[13] in war,
their *vikretas*[14] and their *ryots*.[15]
And then, after all that, we finally became the *munshis*[16] and the lawyers,
the engineers and doctors.
We are never gone.
(This is the lesson.)
You are because we were first.

But if I have a prayer for you, it would be this:
> in your stillness, in the rage of your walking on the sea,
> remember that you are like that banyan tree
> you and I once saw in a Durban park
> (like the one from the Upanishads).

The seed inside you is the invisible origin of the whole spreading tree.
These are the voices of the dead you look for, whose words you want to hear again.
They are inside you.
Open your shell and you will find them.
Their roots seem lost in the mud, but they are what hold up your branches,
and return them to the roots again, and again and again.

---

12. Washerman or woman
13. Soldiers – especially Indian colonial soldiers
14. Seller or vendor
15. Farm worker
16. Teacher

Tat-tvam-asi.
This will become That.
You will become That.
These are all the things you need to know –
my love, my dancer, destroyer and builder –
to go in peace.

IX

(Third Child)

One day, long before I let you come to find me,
when memory is no longer as heavy as these peeling walls,
I will become like Oom Sakkie and Tannie Miems,
dom ou mense.

They sit in the dark lounge here watching TV, their faces blue and contented.
They have stopped wanting to understand anything, or to speak.
The people inside the TV can be switched off,
like the life outside.
They expect nothing from them and give nothing in return.
At 10 every night, they get up and go to bed.
They are happy.

One day I will also expect nothing,
leave the TV and go to bed.

Then, maybe, you can come.

◎ ◎ ◎

There must be a decision, son.
There must be a decision to forgive and to ask to be forgiven,
leaving memory to live its own life at last.

To give, though the giving is not fully understood, or it would not be giving.
To be a servant, both wanted and ridiculed.
To be a master, both wanted and ridiculed.
To put on the masks needed by both, and to know when to let them fall.

Only then can the father honestly say:
>   This is the thing. This is the ultimate thing:
>   to be allowed to know the One who will replace Me.
>   To hold my next life in my hand and let it go
>   through all the doors we have opened and closed,
>   past the final closing, into an unmasked life, beyond doors.

◎ ◎ ◎

My son,
    one of the doors of all my many doors, unsettled eye behind my memories –
this is my decision, behind the door:

I forgive, you forgive, we forgive;
I search, you search, we search, like I searched for you once in the black Klapmuts[17] veld
and in the Cape highway rain; and in the stormy sea-night
when you left to make footprints on the waves;
            and every night between the blank walls of our separate rooms.

---

17. Small town near Cape Town

If you do not forgive, or do not search,
or do not call my name at night or wonder if I call yours –
                I will call anyway, forgive, and wait to be forgiven.

                Forgiveness is home soil.

It is the only ground where your eye and mine can see each other, without doors.

                I will make these my first steps.
              I will walk alone if I must, though without you
                  I do not know the way.

                Without you I can never arrive.

The First Man

III

The Unsettled Amphitheatre

A man rose from the sea beneath the Mountain's amphitheatre; ancient pools
dripped from his limbs, his beard, his worn eyebrows, his salted brown skin.

From his eyes fell worlds yet to come – barbed wire, Ratels, star-walled forts, mine pits,
shopping centres, mansions and pondokkies where trees had been,
tar where elephants had walked, smokestacks where birds had nested;
                          soil and air laced with gold and sulphur and iron.

The pools spread slowly across the town's stone and sod.
                Children played in them.
            Most people packed their things and began to leave.
            No man should have such power, they said.

But the pools began migrating even further over the escarpment
and across the endless veld to the north;
        across the known and the unknown worlds that had never heard of such a man.
And not even when they were drowning, did they think to ask him
                                  why he had done this.

To be healed, to be washed clean,
            to drown and rise again
                (Aristotle said)
a man and a woman must follow the masked
                man and woman strutting the stage,
whose voices echo, unsettled, always unsettled.

To be settled is to die.
To wear the mask is to walk the stage of you and not-you.

The one who thinks they need not move is dead.
    The one who thinks they have found themselves is dead,
their dream kingdom is empty of dreams.

◎ ◎ ◎

"Why so much suffering?" one asked, manacled to the stage
on the rock beside the tree whose blood-flecked leaves could still catch
a suggestion of love.

"Suffering is the purpose of all things," said one.
"Suffering is futile," said another.
"Without suffering there is no relief," said another.
"Suffering serves only itself," said another.

◎ ◎ ◎

To give up trying to outrun your history;
to stop in the sea and let the golden glow of what is given break over you;
to leave the fort and its hard tongue behind in the wake of your own carved words;
to catch, for once, the dawn's mackerel, and be grateful.

These are his desires.

◎ ◎ ◎

A young woman, who was also old, walking on the stage, said:

"I have been down, far down,
to my ancestors, into the dark pits of my history.
I have returned with a summer flower,
but it has wilted in my hand.
Where will I find it again?"

"Only in the pit," said one, old but also young like her.

Blessing

And so, she never stopped her moving, up and down,
up and down, until the way up and the way down became the same,
though they were never in the same place and the flower forever evaded her.

"It is only the flower that keeps you moving," said her old friend.

◎ ◎ ◎

From the pale moon lip of Goa's Calangute the fishing boat *Blessing* –
                              crossed and anointed –
            chugs out into the Arabian Bay's rising gold dawn.

Pedro and Francis, Krishna, Nitesh and Antonio nurse their nets,
as their fathers and fathers' fathers nursed theirs before them.
The sea changes into a sparkle of saffron.
Sea-coins, like fish half a hand long, begin their dance for the nets.

Blessing passes the paragliders, the ski-boats, the paddlers,
leaves the jut of Fort Aguada's old prison jaw pouting in its wake,
and goes right through history –
            the ghosts of Da Gama's and Albuquerque's Caravels
                tonguing the palms, the river, the hills, breaking open roads,
                the honking of horns and scooters,
            and pilgrim crowds pouring through the doors of the Bom Jesus,
            casting, like fishermen, for the golden countenance of Francis Xavier,
                        awaiting his resurrection.

His history is now their history.
In the work of the fishermen's hands is embalmed the desires of centuries –

            "Give us, O Lord, so that we may give in turn,"

And from their silk thread nets at noon they pick the silver sea coins –
pomfret, kingfish and mackerel –
and, like priests, offer them to the wicker baskets:
a sacrament for the sand from what's left of the sea.

It is all they have left to give.

◎ ◎ ◎

Just beyond Algoa Bay's lip, while the *Blessing* is returning to Calangute,
the chokka boats bob their small stars across the waves,
as they have for forty years.
They are the only light of endeavor available to Petrus,
Johannes, Lucas, Dawid and Joseph. They nurse their lines,
like their fathers before them, some now at the bottom of the bay.

The block face of Fort Frederick looks down upon them,
as it did their white ancestors and their Malay and Madagascar slave ancestors.
Cape Recife lighthouse eyes them.

The squall is all they have to live by; they are one story left by the settlers,
forever unsettled in a bay always unquiet.
They have sailed through the ghosts of Da Gama and Diaz, of the Meermin,
and of Baines and Mrs Donkin, still pale and wan in Hindustan.

They think only of today, and their only speech is prayer:

"O Lord, give us our quota of chokka,
so that we may have food
and our children have clothes."

In the dawn their catch is packed, blast frozen, and delivered to Spain for paella.
Then they can go home to their pondokkies to sleep.
They have given what they have left to give.

◎ ◎ ◎

Let me touch you as you once desired to be touched.

Let me oil your thighs, your buttocks, your arms,
your breasts, your korrel khoe hair, with the promise of pomegranates,
and your feet with the gesture of aloes.

Let me call you by the name only you know:
"Ssehura, our Saartjie;
everyone's Saartjie and nobody's Saartjie."

Let me relieve you of the memories they collected,
and the cracked clay wall they left for you in the orchards of Hankey.
Let me tell you that from forgetting, orchards grow.

Let me ….

◎ ◎ ◎

By the waters of the Kei, we sat down and fished.
The grey-bellied Grunters were no match for us white-bellied boys.
Nor was the wrinkled-breasted old woman smoking her pipe on the other bank.

Saartjie

We laughed when King Hintsa's head floated past.
We laughed when the ghosts of the woman's ancestors rose
from the water with their spears because the cattle were dead.
We laughed even when her smoke blackened the river mouth,
and we had to leave for our tents in darkness.

We cooked our catch and drank our beer.
We did not hear what became of the ancestors.
We did not hear what became of the woman.

◎ ◎ ◎

On a long, thin stretch of black road in the desert, a Cadillac had come to a halt.
After a long time, a camel rider came past.

"I need gas," said the man in the Cadillac. "'I will pay you to buy me gas
at the nearest filling station and return to me."

"I have no idea if there are any filling stations nearby," said the camel rider.
"But you can come with me to where I am going."

"I am not going where you are going. And besides, I eat camels. I don't ride them.
They are smelly," said the driver.

The camel rider went on his way.

◎ ◎ ◎

O Raglan Road
raggle on –
up, up, up
to the raggley city on the hill,
where the children play
among their dreams.

Bring them their blades;
bring their brass, their shields and burning bows;
bring their flaming arrows of desire;
bring their cups of molten gold –
so they can raise them to their lips
and drink, and drink and drink
till all their dreams are done.

◎ ◎ ◎

There was one[18] who came from the north to pitch his tent in the spear-sharp bush,
to dream like Jacob dreamed of ladders at Bethel rising from the waters of the veld.
It was a bank to climb on to, and a stage to tell from – of the wife taken in Rotterdam
waters from his arm, and a daughter stolen by the river's mouth.
In the veld, they would find him again. And when they did,
they came from the slave waters of Madagascar to be sold.
They became his ladders when he bought them; his house when he set them free.
He said, "What was taken has been returned.
Those who refused to be forgotten, have never left."

His tongue learned Khoe clicks.
His wife and children became a multitude.
Histories rose from the rivers of grief.

---

18. Dr J T van der Kemp, missionary and founder of Bethelsdorp

Long after he was gone,
their sons returned to the water to be fishermen,
their daughters to the cities to build memories.

But he never forgot his grief.

◎ ◎ ◎

"I will walk with you on the shopping mall marble, under the fluorescence of the things you have collected and in which you believe," the man, the First Man,
who had risen from the sea, said.
"If you want, I can show you that these things are not yourself, but only shells echoing memories you wish you had."

"We are happy with the memories we have made," said one.
"They are our own minds' fluorescence, and they are the marble of our powers."

"Of course, they are not enough," said another.
"But we can accept them as enough, can't we?"

"What is the point of always wanting more, more, more?" said a third.
"We are sick of wanting, now. Up and down, up and down, world wandering. Leave us with our own creations and our own memories."

◎ ◎ ◎

Under the old slave bell in Bethelsdorp, Jermaine, self-proclaimed head of the Mongrels of this spot, hangs a tattooed arm, furrows a tattooed brow, for the tourists.
Pay him a fifty for a pic, he'll show you a gangster face, drop some gap-toothed Tsotsi taal.

> "Dis, dis who we are, my bra.
> We, the people, we the heroes of our struggle.
> Nie *boemelaars*, nee nee. Heroes. Without us, the people starve.
> Dagga and Tik is mos staples."

He wears the cross on his cheek like a warning.

> "Dis, Dis is my blessing. I live by it, mos."

It is the shape of a knife, pointing up and down,
> down and up,
>> east and west.

◎ ◎ ◎

The man who had come from the sea, the First Man,
stood in the pools he had brought and was sad.
He wished for a different outcome: maskless, transparent, clear,
> of humble and generous intent;
>> an outcome to bathe in, unflecked.

To begin again, he said, to return to the sea and begin again,
> and again and again,
>> time without end,
>>> is the only outcome worthy of endeavor.

> He would take the first step.
>> His feet would make prints on the water for others to follow.
>> His words would be the comfort of familiar feet.

From the southern lip of the amphitheatre, into the misty veil of the sea,
he began to walk with the chokka boats;
> and from the northern lip beside the *Blessing* riding into the golden sun,
>> he began to walk.

Kevin Goddard grew up in the mining town of Welkom in the Free State. After studying, first theology, then literature, in what was then Grahamstown, now Makhanda, he began lecturing at Vista university in Gqeberha in the early '90s. He migrated to NMMU (now Nelson Mandela University) in 2004 then left to take up work in Saudi Arabia in 2010. He and his wife Sheena both taught and lived in KSA for twelve years but have now returned to Gqeberha where he is a research fellow at the Centre for Gender and African Studies, UFS.

Kevin has published a number of poems in South African magazines as well as academic articles locally and internationally. This is his first book of poems.

Botsotso Poetry since 2016

Songs of Tenderness and Dread – Abu Bakr Solomons

Loud and Yellow Laughter – Sindiswa Bususku-Mathese

The Colours of Our Flag – Allan Kolski Horwitz

The Alkalinity of Bottled Water – Makhosazana Xaba

On Days Such as This – Gail Dendy

Inhibiting Love – Abu Bakr Solomons

A History of Disappearance – Sarah Lubala

Hungry on Arrival – Kabelo Mofokeng

U Grand, Malume? – Sizakele Nkosi

Zabalaza Republic – Sihle Ntuli

Studies in Khoisan Verbs and other poems – Basil du Toit

Everybody is a Bridge – Anton Krueger

Igoli Egoli – Salimah Valiani

Down the Baakens Underworld – Brian Walter

A place to night in – Frank Meintjies

Flight of the Bird Spirit – Richard Cullinan

Maxwell the Gorilla and the Archbishop of Soshanguve – Angifi Proctor Dlaldla (on the Botsotso website)

Notes from the Dream Kingdom – KG Goddard

Rubble – Abu Bakr Solomons

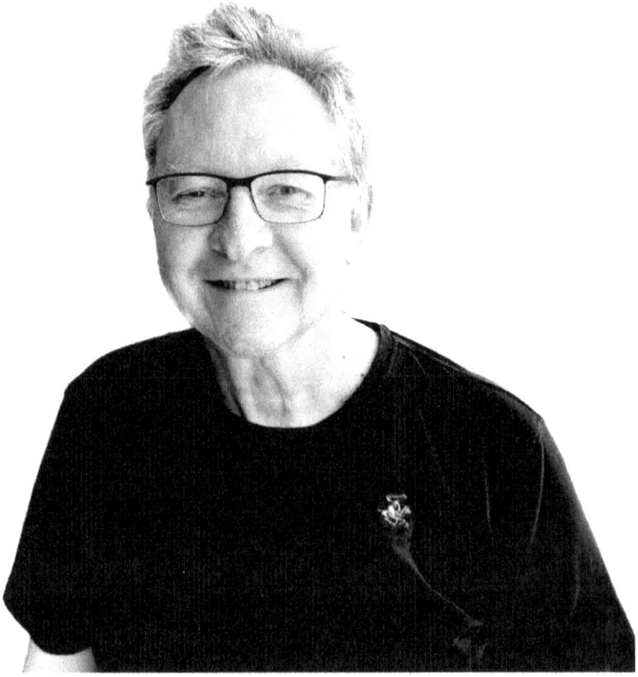